I-SPY

with David Bellamy

TREES

I-Spy Books
12 Star Road, Partridge Green
Horsham, Sussex RH13 8RA

What are they called? You don't know? Well, start I-SPYING right now!

The tree on my sweatshirt in the inside front cover picture is an ELM, a very special elm, called SAPPORO AUTUMN GOLD. It has been specially bred by a botanist called Professor Eugene Smalley of the University of Wisconsin in America, and is resistant to the Dutch Elm Disease.

Some of our trees are native, and these are marked with an 'N' in the book. This means that they got here by natural means after the last Ice Age. All the rest have been introduced by man.

Trees are not just beautiful and useful to us, they are high-rise homes for insects, birds, mammals and for other plants.

ALDER (N)

A large shrub, or a tall tree—usually found in nice damp places.

The young branches are smooth, covered with resin warts, and are sticky.

Young bark is smooth and shiny and greenish-brown; old bark is dark grey and rugged.

If you touch the young leaf you could describe its texture in one word.

What is that word?..Score 25

ASH, the last of our native trees to unfold its leaves.

ASH (N)

A very stately, graceful tree. I-SPY lance-shaped leaflets arranged in pairs with a single terminal one. The flowers unfold before the leaves and, by late summer, lots of winged fruits called samaras remain on the tree until winter.

As the Ash casts a light shadow look for bushes and a rich herbage growing under it.

The buds can be seen in winter. What colour are they?
....Score **25**

ASPEN produce a light wood ideal for making matches.

ASPEN (N)

The Aspen is sometimes referred to as the 'quivering' tree. It is a sort of Poplar. I-SPY a small tree with thick, almost circular leaves which appear in May.

The male catkins are light red; the small seeds are covered with cottony down and are easily dispersed by the wind. Flowers appear in March and April. The young bark is smooth and whitish grey; old bark is dark grey and rugged.

Aspen leaves are set quivering by the slightest breeze.

Why do they quiver more easily than other leaves? ......

....Score **30**

Earthworms do not enjoy eating BEECH leaves, green or red.

COPPER BEECH (N)

Leaves and shoots are a light copper colour in spring, then darken gradually during summer. Normally these are propagated by grafting as their seeds usually produce the ordinary Beech.

On young trees, on low branches of old ones, and on clipped hedges you will see some of the dried and withered leaves all through the winter. They fall off just before the new leaves appear.

The young leaves are folded and covered with soft, silky hairs; fully grown leaves are ovate with curved edges.

The amount of fruit, called mast, varies from year to year.

Where did you see your Copper Beech?.................................

....Score **35**

BIRCH brooms are made from birch twigs.

BIRCH (N)

A graceful tree, and hardier than even the Oak. The slender trunk has smooth silvery bark which peels off in thin strips. Leaves are small and roughly triangular; when they open in April they are at first sticky with resin; when this dries it leaves white scales.

The flowers appear a short time after the leaves; the fruit ripens in July.

I-SPY male and female catkins—the male hangs down.

The fruit is a tiny nut with wings.

How many wings? ....

Date seen .... Score **25**

7

I first saw BOX on Box Hill in Surrey.

BOX (N)

An evergreen shrub, or a small tree, often found in chalky districts. I-SPY its long, leathery compound leaves with very small leaflets, dark green above and pale green underneath.

The hard wood of the Box is yellow, heavy and even grained, and very suitable for wood engraving and for making rulers.

The tiny flowers are greenish-white and appear in May. The fruit is a greenish-white capsule holding six small black seeds.

How many leaflets do you find at the tip of each leaf?

....

Where did you see your Box?...........................Score **40**

ELDER fruits are rich in Vitamin C, no wonder the birds like them.

ELDER (N)

A shrub, but can grow into a tree up to 10 metres tall. Very common on roadsides and waste places in towns, especially on the nitrogen-enriched soil of rubbish dumps. I-SPY the deeply furrowed corky bark, and the prominent breathing pores on the young grey wood; the young stems with light white pith which can be removed to produce a good pea-shooter; the creamy-white saucers of scented flowers, being visited by flies in April and May, and the dark scarlet fruits later in the year.

How many main rays make up the saucer of flowers?...

....

.... Score **25**

ELM leaves sometimes sting people.

COMMON ELM (N)

Both these elms are dying from Dutch Elm Disease, carried by a tiny beetle that lives under the bark.

A tall, stately tree. I-SPY small leaves, a straight trunk with one main stem and many suckers or new shoots.

The leaves have stalks about a centimetre long; they unfold and fall later than those of the Wych Elm; they are a beautiful yellow in autumn.

The wood of the Elm is much valued for furniture and coffins; it is strong, tough, impossible to cleave and resistant to salt sea winds. The young branches are covered with hair.

Do you see hairs on the older branches?.................................

....Score **25**

10

Ancient water pipes made from hollowed ELM trunks have been excavated in London.

WYCH ELM (N)

A broad rounded head—or top; spreading lower branches; larger leaves than those of the Common Elm. They are arranged in two rows; have short stalks; are pointed and have rough upper surfaces and downy undersides.

The dark red flowers appear in early spring and develop fruits very quickly. These are large and green and hang in thick clusters, before the leaf buds open.

Were the leaves rough or smooth to the touch? ....

....Score **30**

FALSE ACACIA

Frequently called the Locust Tree. I-SPY fragrant flowers hanging in long plumes and leaves with many pairs of leaflets. More often found in parks and gardens than in woods. From eastern USA.

Recognise it by its domed crown, and its smooth branches with spines, which are strongest in the young shoots but weaker on the top branches. Notice the fruits.

Do the lines in the bark run vertically or in spiral fashion?..Score **40**

FIELD MAPLE (N)

Our first and our only native Maple. A hedge shrub or a small tree. I-SPY its ruddy brown shoots in winter, and its small yellow-green petals in spring. Later its seed pods look like small model gliders.

Young branches are green but quickly become reddish brown, with brown stripes. The buds are small and contain milky juice.

The leaves have downy hair along the veins on the undersides and become bright yellow in autumn.

Is the bark of your Maple smooth and firm, or does it flake away in your hands?...Score **30**

HAZEL (N)

The Hazel is always a bush, with branches growing from the ground. It has brownish or greyish smooth shiny bark. Young shoots are thickly covered with hairs. Leaves are rounded, short-stalked and hairy; they appear in early May and fall in November.

The male flowers are contained in catkins. The small nuts have thick shells and are in lobed husks—in clusters of two to five; they ripen by September and later fall from the husks.

Date seen...Score **30**

HOLLY leaves spread around your vegetable patch help to keep the slugs at bay.

HOLLY (N)

One of our few wild evergreen broad-leaved trees. Can grow into a 20 metres high tree, but is more usually a bush.

The leaves are alternate, hard, leathery; glossy and dark green. Low down on the tree they are waved with strong prickly teeth; higher up they lose their teeth, are often oval and narrower.

Clusters of small, white flowers appear in June; they are usually of one sex on one tree—hence many garden Holly bushes never bear berries. The fruits are coral-red, four-seeded drupes.

What kind of bark had your Holly? .... Score **30**

HORNBEAM (N)

Sometimes mistaken for an Elm or Beech. But it is more spreading than the Elm, and the young leaves are duller than Beech leaves.

Leaves are alternate and in two rows; they are narrow, pointed, deeply serrated and ribbed. They unfold in May, when the flowers appear.

The male flowers come from buds which bear flowers only; the female flowers come from buds which also contain leaves.

The nut is ribbed and is only half-enclosed by a three-lobed wing which becomes a kind of sail when the fruit is dispersed. Find one of the longest leaves on your Hornbeam.

How long is it?..

Date noted..Score **35**

CONKER: I once had a 'hundred and two-er'—how about you?

HORSE CHESTNUT

The 'conker' tree, from the Balkans. Young bark is smooth, older bark peels off in thin flakes.

Leaves are palmate, with 5-7 leaflets; at first they are whitish-yellow, like felt, and hang downwards; when they grow in May they are seen to be doubly serrated; when they fall in autumn they leave large scars on the branches.

The flowers, in cone-shaped clusters, almost cover the tree; the fruit usually contains one large, brown, shiny seed with a large round spot—the 'navel'. Look also for the White Chestnut and the smaller Red Chestnut.

Date noted..Score **25**

LIME (N)

A tall handsome tree, sometimes used to make a beautiful avenue. I-SPY its thin upward-spreading branches, and in late spring its fresh light-green heart-shaped leaves.

The sweet scented flowers of the Lime, growing in clusters of 7 to 11 blooms, are rich in nectar, so in summer they are alive with bees. Don't let the sticky nectar drip on your car!

The seeds from the fruit may sometimes germinate eighteen months after they fall.

What is unusual about the flower stalk of the Lime?......

Where did you see yours?...................................Score **30**

White MULBERRIES were planted around Buckingham Palace to feed Silk Worms.

MULBERRY

This is the Black Mulberry, a small spreading tree. I-SPY its flowers in greenish-white clusters and, later on, its dark red fruit. It lives to a great age, and there are many historic specimens. From W. Asia.

Note the pale, downy under sides of the leaves in contrast to the upper surface.

Where did you see yours?.................... ....Score **50**

OAKS provide a high-rise home and snack bar for more than 300 sorts of insect.

COMMON OAK (N)

A monarch of a tree.

When young the tree has smooth, shiny, greyish bark; with age it becomes rough, furrowed and rugged.

Buds are short and plump. Leaves begin to appear in April, and are out by mid-May. They are pinnately lobed.

Male flowers are enclosed in long, hanging catkins; flowering female catkins—one to five in number—grow upright on fairly long stalks; the fruit is an acorn, enclosed in a cup at the base.

What colour were the twigs of your Oak?..............................

Did your Oak have stalks to each acorn?............Score **25**

HOLM OAK

Smaller than the British Oak; its lower branches often droop almost to the ground, making it look like a huge bush. An evergreen from S. Europe.

I-SPY thick, shiny leaves and branchlets covered with grey felt. The male flowers grow in little clusters on hanging stems; female flowers grow in the axils of the new leaves. It takes about two years for them to mature into acorns, about 2.5 cms long.

Date noted............ ....Score **35**

21

TURKEY OAK

Sometimes called Mossy Cupped Oak. A tall oak, usually pyramid in shape, which is often grown in gardens. From S. Europe and Asia Minor.

I-SPY narrow, dark green leaves and acorns with tiny stalks and mossy cups. The acorns grow in pairs and, until September, are buried in their cups; they lengthen and push out in October.

In winter look for its resting buds, small, sharply pointed, and light brown with long black hairs which make the twigs look untidy. The leaves are long and thin, with pointed lobes.

Where did you see yours?..

When?...Score **45**

22

PLANE by name, its wood is very beautiful and called Lalewood in the trade.

PLANE (N)

Known as the London Plane, It is believed that it originated in England by the European and American Planes interbreeding. A tall tree planted usually in towns. I-SPY a large leaf with five pointed lobes, and conspicuous seed pods like little rough balls. You will often see patches of underbark on the trunk, for in winter the bark peels off. A deciduous tree whose leaves fall off while still green. I-SPY the down on the young leaves.

What colour is it?...

Where did you see your Plane?.............................. Score **30**

What's special about the leaf stalk? A clue—break one open!

23

BALSAM POPLAR

I-SPY this tree in parks and gardens. It grows into a large tree—up to 30 metres, and the bark becomes furrowed at an early age.

The leaves are a dirty yellow underneath and veined like a net.

This tree's resin is scented, contains oils, and is called 'balsam'. A North American.

Which parts of this tree smell of balsam? ....

Where was it growing? .... Score **35**

24

BLACK POPLAR (N)

A wide-spreading tree which can grow to a height of 45 metres with a girth of 9 metres.

I-SPY dark grey bark, and pointed leaves with a broad base. The timber is used for matches, paper pulp and joinery.

How were the leaf-buds of your Black Poplar arranged along the twigs?..Score **40**

LOMBARDY POPLAR

Called 'Lombardy' because it is commonly grown on the Lombardy plains of Northern Italy.

The commonest of the poplar trees, and nearly all those in Britain are male; these are preferred because they do not shed the downy seeds which make gardens look untidy.

Leaves are diamond-shaped and pointed, serrated above the middle, with many glands at the leaf base.

I-SPY its great height and its near vertical branches. No other large tree in this country is like it. Look for it in parks and gardens. The catkins are of two colours.

What are they?..Score **25**

WHITE POPLAR

A tall tree which grows rapidly. I-SPY mottled white patches on the greyish-green bark, and a dense white down on the underside of the leaves. So this tree is well-named. Look for the catkins early in February, and the new leaves and shoots in April.

The leaf stalk is round—not flattened as in other poplars.

You will see many suckers—a disadvantage in a garden, but an advantage where dense, low growth is needed. C. Europe to W. Asia.

Where did you see your White Poplar?...............................
.... Score **30**

ROWAN TREE OR MOUNTAIN ASH (N)

No relative of the Ash tree—though its leaves are rather similar. I-SPY a small tree or large bush with a delicate appearance, creamy-white strong-smelling flowers and lots of berries—coral-red to orange, and containing three seeds.

Leaves unfold as early as mid-April; flowers appear in May; fruit ripens in August.

What do you notice about the leaf-stalk? ....

.... Score **25**

There are more than 300 different sorts of WILLOW in the world.

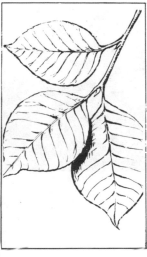

SALLOW (N)

Sometimes called Goat Willow because the leaves were eaten by domestic goats, especially in spring. The large leaves have smooth, dark green upper surfaces and greyish-white felted under surfaces.

The catkins come out early, and the yellow pollen on the male ones make them very easily seen. Female catkins are greenish-yellow and not so conspicuous.

Date noted.. Score **40**

29

WILD SERVICE TREE (N)

This bush or small tree has plump shiny green buds, and wide leaves with 5-7 pointed lobes. These leaves are downy when young, smooth and hairless later on, and blood red in autumn.

Flowers are white; the fruit is round or oval, leathery brown when ripe and dotted with cork pores, sweet enough to be eaten raw and used by the Romans in medicine.

Where did you see yours growing?..

....Score **50**

30

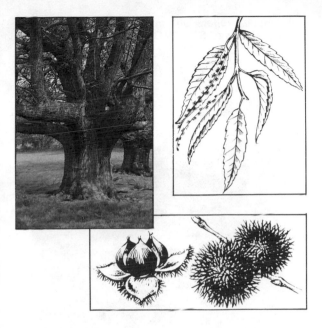

SWEET CHESTNUT

The true chestnut—you can roast and eat the nuts. I-SPY deep channels in the bark arranged spirally, and long toothed leaves with an outline like the blade of a spear; they are mid-green in colour and turn bright brown as they wither. From the Mediterranean.

Male catkins appear in July; smaller female catkins quickly ripen to nuts which fall in November. They mature only in southern England. The spines on the husk are soft but very prickly; the fruit is oval and splits into three nuts.

Date noted .... Score **35**

The wooden rollers on your granny's mangle were probably made of SYCAMORE.

SYCAMORE

A tall tree of the Maple family. I-SPY large lobed leaves, and seed-pods with twin wings. The parts which bear the seeds are domed. Old bark is light greyish-brown and peels off in large flakes; leaves have dark green uppersides and pale bluish-green undersides; flowers unfold in May and hang in long, green clusters. From Europe and W. Asia.

What often spoils the appearance of the leaves in late summer?..Score **30**

TULIP TREES were introduced from the USA where they grow 60 metres tall.

TULIP TREE

A magnificent spreading tree, found in parks and gardens

I-SPY its large saddle-shaped leaves, and its cup-shaped flowers—variegated in green, yellow and orange.

In what way is the bark on the trunk different from that on the branches? ....Score **45**

WHITEBEAM (N)

So-called because of the white colour of the underside of the leaves. 'Beam' is an Anglo-Saxon word for tree.

A rare tree of the Apple family. I-SPY in spring its conspicuous white colour—a white silky down on the leaves and shoots. I-SPY the fruits—like large marbles, in late summer. Whitebeam fruit is red, but usually there is another conspicuous marking.

What was the skin-colouring on yours?.................................

When did you see it?.................................

Can you think of another tree with 'beam' in its name?

.................................Score **45**

WILD CHERRY (N)

I-SPY several varieties of cherry used for ornamental purposes. Their flowers vary from white to red and are beautiful, but the tiny and bitter fruits are inedible—except, of course, for birds!

The bark is greyish-brown—smooth and shiny when young, but ragged when older. The horizontal stripes you see on it are lenticels—breathing pores.

What colour fruit did your Wild Cherry bear? ....
.... Score **35**

35

WILLOWS are pollinated by insects, not wind. Take a look at the catkins.

CRACK WILLOW (N)

The name 'crack' is said to refer to this tree's brittle-ness.

It can grow up to 15 metres high, with an open crown and wide-spreading branches—easily broken by the wind.

Leaves are lance-shaped, smooth and hairless; on the dull light-green upper surfaces small grey spots can be seen under a magnifying glass. The undersides are pale grey. Look out for it along river banks.

Where did you see yours?..Score **30**

WHITE WILLOW (N)

I-SPY a white down on the under surface of the leaf. So, when the leaves move in the wind, the tree has a bright silvery appearance. Hence the name, White Willow.

The thin branches cut from a pollarded willow are used in making baskets and hurdles.

There are many varieties of White Willow, the most common being those with pendulous branches— Weeping Willow, Hanging Willow. Another variety has shoots in winter that are bright red.

Look for any variety of White Willow along roadsides and fences and in parks and gardens.

Describe the bark of your White Willow in two words

....Score **30**

JUNIPER (N)

A fir-like conifer found often on chalky soil, and sometimes as a shrub in gardens. The fruit is a berry and not a cone, composed of fleshy scales fused together. They take two years to ripen—bluish-green in the first year, dark blue with a white waxy coating in the second.

The needles are tapering, awl-shaped and grow in threes—bluish-green on top, dark green beneath.

Male and female flowers are found only on separate trees; male flowers are yellow and easy to see; female flowers are greenish and inconspicuous.

How many scales did the berry have?...................................

Where did you find your Juniper?...................................

...................................Score **40**

38

SCOTS PINE (N)

This native conifer has bluish-green needles arranged in pairs; single needles are found only on saplings.

The male flowers produce a lot of pollen in May, then die and fall off, leaving a bare patch.

The female flowers are red, as small as peas.

Cones take about three years to mature, then the seeds fall out in dry spring weather.

Old bark is thick and scaly, blackish-brown at the base of the tree; higher up it is thinner and bright reddish-yellow, peeling off like paper in flakes.

What was growing under the tree?

....Score **30**

39

YEW wood put the power in the English Long Bow.

YEW (N)

This evergreen conifer may grow as a thick bush up to 3 metres high, or as a tree up to 30 metres.

Needles are dark green and glossy on the upper side, light green and dull on the underside.

Male flowers come from large globular buds on the undersides of the shoots, female flowers from smaller ovoid buds. Notice the seeds.

Date seen... Score **25**

DOUGLAS FIR

Named after David Douglas, a Scottish plant hunter
and an explorer of North America, from where this
tree was introduced only in 1927. Despite this,
specimens already 55 metres tall have been recorded
in Britain—a magnificent forest tree. Distinguished
from all other conifers by its drooping oval cylindrical
cones which have long pointed bracts sticking up
between the woody scales.

How many points were there on the bracts?........................

How tall was your Douglas Fir?—a guesstimate will

do ....Score **45**

LARCH

Can grow to a height of 50 metres. The bark is greyish-brown, shed in small plates. 30 to 40 bright green needle leaves on each shoot, which are dropped in autumn—yes, this is a deciduous conifer. The young cones are bright pink, rarely cream, in March and April, and the mature cones are produced in September and can remain on the tree for some years. Introduced from the Alps and Carpathians it is grown as a forestry tree and gives a pleasant variation to the large, otherwise evergreen plantations.

How long were the cones?..

Where did you see the tree?..Score **40**

Britain's tallest tree is a GRAND FIR, measured at 57 metres and still growing.

LAWSON CYPRESS

Lawson was a Scottish nurseryman who sent Murray the botanist to explore North America for rare trees. This tree, like the Douglas Fir, comes from Western North America.

I-SPY the single tapering trunk of this tall conifer with short horizontal branches, and its dense twigs. The cones are small and rounded with woody cone scales shaped like a shield.

The shoots are fine and narrow; the upper sides are green and the undersides have irregular whitish markings.

What colour are the cones?...Score **40**

Britain's largest forest is the Kielder in Northumberland.

SILVER FIR

A tall tree—can grow to a height of 60 metres. You can identify it by the flat, spread-out branches and very short, thick green needles with two white stripes on the undersides—these provide the 'silver' of the name. From Europe. The Christmas Tree.

I-SPY the male flowers, like short catkins, on the previous year's shoot; the female flowers are upright and grow singly.

The cones are erect and when ripe disintegrate into seeds, cone scales and bracts.

About how long were the needles?......................Score **45**

Britain needs more trees desperately. Would you like to help plant some, or how about a school tree project? Write to me, Chief I-Spy, and I will pass your letter on.

SPRUCE

Is sometimes called 'spruce fir'. There are several forms of this tree, but on them all I-SPY green needles with a diamond-shaped cross-section; and many smaller side branches. From N. and C. Europe.

Flowers come out in May—the red female ones first in the top of the crown, then the male ones in the middle and bottom of the crown. These male flowers produce so much pollen that the ground below is often yellow with 'sulphur rain'.

The cones have leathery rounded cone scales and grow up to 8 cms long.

Date noted................................ ....Score **35**

On holiday in Scotland?—then go to see Britain's oldest tree, a Yew, in Fortingall, near Aberfeldy.

WELLINGTONIA

The Giant Redwood Tree from America. I-SPY its tall straight trunk, its spire-like shape, with wide spreading lower branches, tapering to shorter ones.

The bark is thick, soft and spongy; the leaves are short, pointed shiny green spikes.

Look, in May, for the pale fresh green new shoots contrasting with the old leaves.

It takes two years for the cone to reach its full size—about 5 cm long; in the second autumn the scales open and release the seeds.

What colour was the bark of your Wellingtonia?.................

....Score **40**

JOIN THE I-SPY CLUB

- All you need to join the I-SPY Club is to buy a Membership Book which includes the secret codes. Ask at your bookshop or newsagent.

- Tell your friends about I-SPY. Invite them to join and form a Patrol with you.

- Collect all the I-SPY books—and you'll have a wonderful library of your own.

- Write to me about any interesting discoveries you make. You may win a prize! Remember to enclose a stamped addressed envelope for a reply.

LOOK OUT FOR THESE I-SPY WITH DAVID BELLAMY BOOKS

AT THE AIRPORT	ON A CAR JOURNEY
ARCHAEOLOGY	CAR NUMBERS
AT THE ART GALLERY	CARS
BIRDS AND REPTILES AT THE ZOO	CIVIL AIRCRAFT DINOSAURS
BRITISH COINS	GARDEN BIRDS

AND MANY **MORE!** TO COME

INDEX

The Government department concerned with trees is:-
The Forestry Commission, 25 Corstorphine Road, Edinburgh.

Societies include:-
The Royal Forestry Society of England, Wales and Northern Ireland, 102 High Street, Tring, Herts; The Royal Scottish Forestry Society, 18 Abercrombie Place, Edinburgh; Men of the Trees, Crawley Down, Crawley, Sussex; The Tree Council, 35 Belgrave Square, London SW1X 8QN.

I-Spy thank Alan F. Mitchell for his assistance and photos. Others courtesy of Biofotos and the Harry Smith Picture collection. 'Shell Times' for David Bellamy's photograph on page 2. Series Editor Anthony Maynard.

Published by Ravette Limited, 12 Star Road, Partridge Green, Horsham, West Sussex RH13 8RA © Ravette Ltd. 1983. Printed in Italy (KEL)
ISBN 0-906710-33-2